To

_____

From

_____

Date

_____

PRAYERS

of a *Loyal Friend*

FOURTH EDITION

PRAYERS

of a *Loyal Friend*

The quoted ideas expressed in this book (but not Scripture verses) are not, in all cases, exact quotations, as some have been edited for clarity and brevity. In all cases, the author has attempted to maintain the speaker's original intent. In some cases, quoted material for this book was obtained from secondary sources, primarily print media. While every effort was made to ensure the accuracy of these sources, the accuracy cannot be guaranteed. For additions, deletions, corrections, or clarifications in future editions of this text, please write Brighton Books.

Scripture quotations are taken from:

The Holy Bible, King James Version

The Holy Bible, New International Version (NIV) Copyright © 1973, 1978, 1984, by International Bible Society. Used by permission of Zondervan Publishing House. All rights reserved.

The Holy Bible, New King James Version (NKJV) Copyright © 1982 by Thomas Nelson, Inc. Used by permission.

The New American Standard Bible®, (NASB) Copyright © 1960, 1962, 1963, 1968, 1971, 1972, 1973, 1975, 1977, 1995 by The Lockman Foundation. Used by permission.

The Holy Bible, New Living Translation, (NLT) Copyright © 1996. Used by permission of Tyndale House Publishers, Inc., Wheaton, Illinois 60189. All rights reserved.

New Century Version®. (NCV) Copyright © 1987, 1988, 1991 by Word Publishing, a division of Thomas Nelson, Inc. All rights reserved. Used by permission.

The Message (MSG)- This edition issued by contractual arrangement with NavPress, a division of The Navigators, U.S.A. Originally published by NavPress in English as THE MESSAGE: The Bible in Contemporary Language copyright 2002-2003 by Eugene Peterson. All rights reserved.

The Holman Christian Standard Bible™ (HCSB) Copyright © 1999, 2000, 2001 by Holman Bible Publishers. Used by permission.

Cover Design by Kim Russell / Wahoo Designs
Page Layout by Bart Dawson

ISBN 1-58334-244-3

Printed in the United States of America

Table of Contents

Introduction

*L*oyal Christian friendship is ordained by God. Throughout the Bible, we are reminded to love one another, to care for one another, and to treat one another as we wish to be treated. This collection of devotional readings is a celebration of Christian friendship. As such, it is intended to help you in your efforts to be the kind of friend that God intends.

Perhaps you received this book as a gift from a trusted companion, or perhaps you picked it up on your own. Either way, you will be blessed if you take the words of these pages to heart. This text addresses 31 topics. Each brief chapter contains Bible verses, a brief devotional reading, quotations from noted Christian thinkers, and a prayer. The ideas in each chapter are powerful reminders of God's commandments and of the joys of Christian friendship.

Because you have taken time to open this book and begin reading it, you understand the important role that Christian friendship plays in God's plans for His kingdom *and* for your life. Christ promises His followers a life of abundance (John 10:10). May your friends bless you abundantly, and may you do the same for them.

CHAPTER 1

The Joys of Friendship

*Beloved, if God so loved us,
we also ought to love one another.*
1 John 4:11 NKJV

What is a friend? The dictionary defines the word *friend* as "a person who is attached to another by feelings of affection or personal regard." This definition is accurate, as far as it goes, but when we examine the deeper meaning of friendship, so many more descriptors come to mind: trustworthiness, loyalty, helpfulness, kindness, encouragement, understanding, forgiveness, humor, and cheerfulness, to mention but a few.

Genuine friendship should be treasured, protected, and nourished. And how do we do so? By observing the Golden Rule: As Christians, we are commanded to treat others as we wish to be treated (Matthew 7:12). When we treat others with kindness, courtesy, and respect, we build friendships that can last a lifetime. And God smiles.

Do you want to have trustworthy, encouraging friends? Then be one. And make no mistake: that's exactly the kind of friend that God wants you to be.

Friendship is the greatest of worldly goods.
Certainly to me it is the chief happiness of life.
If I had to give a piece of advice to a young
man about a place to live, I think I should say,
"sacrifice almost everything to live
where you can be near your friends."
I know I am very fortunate in that respect.

C. S. Lewis

The bond of human friendship has a sweetness
of its own, binding many souls together as one.

St. Augustine

In friendship, God opens your eyes
to the glories of Himself.

Joni Eareckson Tada

Don't bypass the potential for meaningful
friendships just because of differences.
Explore them. Embrace them. Love them.

Luci Swindoll

Here is a simple, rule-of-thumb for behavior:
Ask yourself what you want people to do for you,
then grab the initiative and do it for them.
Add up God's Law and Prophets
and this is what you get.

—

Matthew 7:12 MSG

A Prayer for Today

Dear Lord, I thank You for the joys of friendship. You have brought wonderful Christian friends into my life. Let me enrich their lives in the same way that they have enriched mine. And let us all glorify You as we follow in the footsteps of Your Son.

—

Amen

CHAPTER 2

Praying for Our Friends

Be kindly affectionate to one another with brotherly love, in honor giving preference to one another; not lagging in diligence, fervent in spirit, serving the Lord; rejoicing in hope, patient in tribulation, continuing steadfastly in prayer.

Romans 12:10-12 NKJV

*J*esus made it clear to His disciples: they should pray always. And so should we. Genuine, heartfelt prayer changes things, and it changes us. When we lift our hearts to our Father in heaven, we open ourselves to a never-ending source of divine wisdom, limitless power, and infinite love.

Today, we offer a prayer of thanks to God for our friends. Loyal Christian friends have much to offer us: encouragement, faith, fellowship, and fun, for starters. And when we align ourselves with godly believers, we are blessed by them *and* by our Creator.

Let us thank God for *all* the people who love us—for the family and friends whom He has placed along our paths. And let's pray for our family and friends with sincere hearts. God hears our prayers, and He responds.

Your family and friends need your prayers
and you need theirs. And God wants to hear
those prayers. So what are you waiting for?

Marie T. Freeman

There is no way that Christians,
in a private capacity, can do so much to
promote the work of God and advance
the kingdom of Christ as by prayer.

Jonathan Edwards

Let's please God by actively seeking,
through prayer, "peaceful and quiet lives"
for ourselves, our spouses, our children and
grandchildren, our friends, and our nation
(1 Timothy 2:1-3 NIV).

Shirley Dobson

Prayer is never the least we can do;
it is always the most!

A. W. Tozer

> *Therefore, let everyone who is godly pray to You.*
>
> —
>
> Psalm 32:6 NASB

A Prayer for Today

Dear Lord, make me a person whose constant
prayers are pleasing to You. Let me come to
You often with concerns both great and small.
I trust in the power of prayer, Father, because
prayer changes things, and it changes me.
In the quiet moments of the day, I will open
my heart to You. I know that You are with me
always and that You always hear my prayers.
So I will pray and be thankful.

—

Amen

CHAPTER 3

Above and Beyond Worry

I have told you these things, so that in me you may have peace. In this world you will have trouble. But take heart! I have overcome the world.

John 16:33 NIV

ere's a riddle: What is it that is too unimportant to pray about yet too big for God to handle? The answer, of course, is: "nothing." Yet sometimes, when the challenges of the day seem overwhelming, we may spend more time worrying about our troubles than praying about them. And, we may spend more time fretting about our problems than solving them. A far better strategy is to pray as if everything depended entirely upon God and to work as if everything depended entirely upon us.

What we see as problems God sees as opportunities. And if we are to trust Him completely, we must acknowledge that even when our own vision is dreadfully impaired, His vision is perfect.

Today and every day, let us trust God by courageously confronting the things that *we* see as problems and *He* sees as possibilities. And while we're at it, let's remind our friends and family members that no problem is too big for God . . . not even *our* problems.

We sometimes fear to bring our troubles to
God because we think they must seem small to
Him. But, if they are large enough to vex and
endanger our welfare, they are large enough
to touch His heart of love.

R. A. Torrey

When considering the size of your problems,
there are two categories that you should never
worry about: the problems that are small
enough for you to handle, and the ones
that aren't too big for God to handle.

Marie T. Freeman

Often the trials we mourn are really gateways
into the good things we long for.

Hannah Whitall Smith

Measure the size of the obstacles against
the size of God.

Beth Moore

Then they cried out to the LORD in their trouble,
and He saved them out of their distresses.

—

Psalm 107:13 NKJV

A Prayer for Today

Lord, sometimes my problems are simply
too big for me, but they are never too big for
You. Let me turn my troubles over to You, Lord,
and let me trust in You today
and for all eternity.

—

Amen

CHAPTER 4

Today Is the Day!

This is the day the LORD has made;
we will rejoice and be glad in it.
Psalm 118:24 NKJV

What do you expect from the day ahead? Are you expecting God to do wonderful things for you, for your family, and for your friends? Or are you living beneath a cloud of apprehension and doubt? The familiar words of Psalm 118:24 remind us of a profound yet simple truth: "This is the day which the LORD hath made; we will rejoice and be glad in it" (KJV).

For Christian believers, every day begins and ends with God and His Son. Christ came to this earth to give us abundant life and eternal salvation. We give thanks to our Maker when we treasure each day and use it to the fullest.

Today, let us give thanks for the gift of life and for the One who created it. And then, let's use this day—a precious gift from the Father above—to serve our Savior and to share His Good News with all who cross our paths.

Commitment to His lordship on Easter,
at revivals, or even every Sunday is not enough.
We must choose this day—and every day—
whom we will serve. This deliberate act of
the will is the inevitable choice between
habitual fellowship and habitual failure.

Beth Moore

Today is mine. Tomorrow is none of my
business. If I peer anxiously into the fog of
the future, I will strain my spiritual eyes so that
I will not see clearly what is required of me now.

Elisabeth Elliot

Each day, each moment is so pregnant
with eternity that if we "tune in" to it,
we can hardly contain the joy.

Gloria Gaither

Wherever you are, be all there.
Live to the hilt every situation
you believe to be the will of God.

Jim Elliot

Encourage one another daily,
as long as it is Today . . . .

—

Hebrews 3:13 NIV

A Prayer for Today

Dear Lord, You have given me another day
of life; let me celebrate this day, and let me
use it according to Your plan. I come to You
today with faith in my heart and praise on
my lips. I praise You, Father, for the gift of life
and for the friends and family members
who make my life rich. Enable me to live
each moment to the fullest,
totally involved in Your will.

—

Amen

CHAPTER 5

Character Counts

Till I die, I will not deny my integrity.
I will maintain my righteousness and
never let go of it; my conscience will not
reproach me as long as I live.

Job 27:5-6 NIV

*H*onesty is the best policy, but it is not always the easiest policy. Sometimes, the truth hurts, and sometimes, it's tough to be a person of integrity . . . tough, but essential.

Billy Graham observed, "Integrity is the glue that holds our way of life together. We must constantly strive to keep our integrity intact. When wealth is lost, nothing is lost; when health is lost, something is lost; when character is lost, all is lost." Loyal friends agree.

Integrity is built slowly over a lifetime. It is the sum of every right decision and every honest word. It is forged on the anvil of honorable work and polished by the twin virtues of honesty and fairness. Integrity is a precious thing—difficult to build but easy to tear down. As believers in Christ, we must seek to live each day with discipline, honesty, and faith. When we do, integrity becomes a habit. And God smiles.

Maintaining your integrity in a world of sham
is no small accomplishment.

Wayne Oates

Image is what people think we are;
integrity is what we really are.

John Maxwell

God never called us to naïveté.
He called us to integrity . . . .
The biblical concept of integrity emphasizes
mature innocence not childlike ignorance.

Beth Moore

There's nothing like the power of integrity.
It is a characteristic so radiant, so steady,
so consistent, so beautiful, that it makes
a permanent picture in our minds.

Franklin Graham

The righteous man walks in his integrity;
his children are blessed after him.

—

Proverbs 20:7 NKJV

A Prayer for Today

Dear Lord, let me be a faithful friend to others,
and let me be an example of righteous behavior
to my friends, to my family, and to the world.
I thank You, Lord, for friends who challenge
me to become a better person; let me do
the same for them today and every day.

—

Amen

CHAPTER 6

The Right Kind of Attitude

*Therefore, since Christ suffered in his body,
arm yourselves also with the same attitude,
because he who has suffered in his body is done
with sin. As a result, he does not live the rest
of his earthly life for evil human desires,
but rather for the will of God.*

1 Peter 4:1-2 NIV

How will you direct your thoughts today? Will you obey the words of Philippians 4:8 by dwelling upon those things that are honorable, true, and worthy of praise? Or will you allow your thoughts to be hijacked by the negativity that seems to dominate our troubled world? Are you fearful, angry, bored, or worried? Are you so preoccupied with the concerns of this day that you fail to thank God for the promise of eternity? Are you confused, bitter, or pessimistic? If so, God wants to have a little talk with you.

God intends that you experience joy and abundance, and He wants you *to share* your blessings with family and friends. So, today and every day hereafter, celebrate this life that God has given you by focusing your thoughts and your energies upon "whatever is of good repute." Today, count your blessings instead of your hardships. And thank the Giver of all things good for gifts that are simply too numerous to count.

Attitude is an inward feeling expressed
by behavior.

John Maxwell

The purity of motive determines
the quality of action.

Oswald Chambers

Outlook determines outcome and
attitude determines action.

Warren Wiersbe

A positive attitude will have positive results
because attitudes are contagious.

Zig Ziglar

*All the days of the oppressed are miserable,
but a cheerful heart has a continual feast.*

———

Proverbs 15:15 HCSB

A Prayer for Today

Lord, I have so many reasons to be thankful;
let my attitude be a reflection of the many
blessings I have received. Make me a loyal,
encouraging friend whose thoughts
are Christlike and whose hopes
are worthy of the One who has
given me so much.

—

Amen

CHAPTER 7

Practical Christianity

Be cheerful no matter what; pray all the time;
thank God no matter what happens.
This is the way God wants you
who belong to Christ Jesus to live.
1 Thessalonians 5:16-18 MSG

*I*f we are to be loyal Christian friends, we must do our best to ensure that our actions are accurate reflections of our beliefs. Our theology must be demonstrated, not only by our words but, more importantly, by our actions. In short, we should be practical believers, quick to act whenever we see an opportunity to serve God.

Are you the kind of practical Christian who is willing to dig in and do what needs to be done when it needs to be done? If so, congratulations: God acknowledges your service and blesses it. But if you find yourself more interested in the fine points of theology than in the needs of your neighbors, it's time to rearrange your priorities. God needs believers who are willing to roll up their sleeves and go to work for Him. Count yourself among that number. Theology is a good thing unless it interferes with God's work. And it's up to you to make certain that *your* theology doesn't.

Christianity, if false, is of no importance, and if true, of infinite importance. The only thing it cannot be is moderately important.

C. S. Lewis

Being a Christian means accepting the terms of creation, accepting God as our maker and redeemer, and growing day by day into an increasingly glorious creature in Christ, developing joy, experiencing love, maturing in peace.

Eugene Peterson

The cross that Jesus commands you and me to carry is the cross of submissive obedience to the will of God, even when His will includes suffering and hardship and things we don't want to do.

Anne Graham Lotz

Christianity, in its purest form, is nothing more than seeing Jesus. Christian service, in its purest form, is nothing more than imitating him whom we see. To see his Majesty and to imitate him . . . that is the sum of Christianity.

Max Lucado

*Now if we have died with Christ,
we believe that we shall also live with Him.*

—

Romans 6:8 HCSB

A Prayer for Today

Dear Lord, You are my sovereign God.
Your Son defeated death; He overcame
the world; He gives me life abundant.
Your Holy Spirit comforts and guides me.
Let me celebrate all Your gifts,
and make me a committed Christian today
and every day that I live.

—

Amen

My Thoughts & Prayers
from This Week

_____

_____

_____

_____

_____

_____

_____

_____

_____

_____

_____

_____

_____

_____

_____

_____

_____

_____

_____

_____

_____

My Thoughts & Prayers
for Next Week

CHAPTER 8

The Power of Encouragement

So encourage each other and give each other
strength, just as you are doing now.

1 Thessalonians 5:11 NCV

*P*art of the art of friendship is learning the skill of encouraging others. And make no mistake: Encouragement is a skill that is learned over time and improved with constant use. As Christians, we are called upon to encourage one another, but sometimes we're not sure exactly what to say or do. How, we ask, can we be most encouraging? The answer is found, in part, by reminding ourselves what genuine encouragement is and what it is not.

The dictionary defines *encouragement* as "the act of inspiring courage and confidence." As Christians, we must first seek to inspire others' confidence in God and in His Son Jesus Christ. We are comforted by the knowledge that God's gifts are too numerous to count and that His love extends to all generations—including our own. While our greatest encouragement comes from the assurance of God's power and His promises, we can also find encouragement when we are reminded of our own abilities and strengths. Genuine encouragement is not idle flattery; it is simply a firm reminder of talents that God has given each of us and of our need to use those talents wisely.

Genuine encouragement should never be confused with pity. God intends for His children to lead lives of abundance, joy, celebration, and praise—not lives of self-pity or regret. So we must guard ourselves against hosting or joining the "pity parties" that so often accompany difficult times. Instead, we must encourage each other to have faith—first in God and His only begotten Son—and then in our own abilities to use the talents God has given us for the furtherance of His kingdom and for the betterment of our own lives.

A single word, if spoken in a friendly spirit,
may be sufficient to turn one
from dangerous error.

Fanny Crosby

A hug is the ideal gift . . . one size fits all.

Anonymous

Do not let any unwholesome talk come out of your mouths, but only what is helpful for building others up according to their needs, that it may benefit those who listen.

—

Ephesians 4:29 NIV

A Prayer for Today

Dear Heavenly Father, because I am Your child, I am blessed. You have loved me eternally, cared for me faithfully, and saved me through the gift of Your Son Jesus. Just as You have lifted me up, Lord, let me lift up others in a spirit of encouragement and optimism and hope. And, if I can help a fellow traveler, even in a small way, Dear Lord, may the glory be Yours.

—

Amen

CHAPTER 9

Beyond
Disappointment

You will be sad, but your sadness will become joy.
John 16:20 NCV

hroughout the seasons of life, we must all endure life-altering personal losses that leave us breathless. When we do, God stands ready to protect us. Psalm 147 promises, "He heals the brokenhearted, and binds their wounds" (v. 3 NASB). When we are troubled, we can call upon our Heavenly Father, and—in His own time and according to His own plan—He will heal us.

Sometimes, of course, it is not us, but instead our friends, who face adversity. When friends or family members face troubling times, our mission is simple: We must assist them in any way we can, either with an encouraging word, a helping hand, or a heartfelt prayer.

Vance Havner had practical advice for Christian friends of every generation. He advised, "No journey is complete that does not lead through some dark valleys. We can properly comfort others only with the comfort we ourselves have been given by God." Let us use our own adversities, then, to comfort others and, by doing so, give glory to One who first comforted us.

The enemy of our souls loves to taunt us with past failures, wrongs, disappointments, disasters, and calamities. And if we let him continue doing this, our life becomes a long and dark tunnel, with very little light at the end.

Charles Swindoll

If your hopes are being disappointed just now, it means that they are being purified.

Oswald Chambers

The next time you're disappointed, don't panic. Don't give up. Just be patient and let God remind you he's still in control.

Max Lucado

Why should I ever resist any delay or disappointment, any affliction or oppression or humiliation, when I know God will use it in my life to make me like Jesus and to prepare me for heaven?

Kay Arthur

There is a time for everything, and everything on earth has its special season.
There is a time to cry and a time to laugh.
There is a time to be sad and a time to dance.

—

Ecclesiastes 3:1,4 NCV

A Prayer for Today

Dear Lord, You are my strength in times of adversity. When I am troubled, You comfort me. When I am discouraged, You lift me up. Whatever my circumstances, Lord, let me trust Your plan for my life. And, when my family and friends are troubled, let me remind them of Your love, Your wisdom, and Your grace.

—

Amen

CHAPTER 10

Forgiveness

*Then Peter came to him and asked,
"Lord, how often should I forgive someone
who sins against me? Seven times?"
"No!" Jesus replied, "seventy times seven!"*

Matthew 18:21-22 NLT

*J*f we wish to build lasting friendships, we must learn how to forgive. Why? Because even our most beloved friends are imperfect (as are we).

Finding the generosity to forgive others is seldom easy, but if we truly desire to obey God's Word, we must learn to forgive our friends and family members, just as we wish to be forgiven by them. Until we learn the art of forgiveness, we remain trapped in prisons of our own resentment and regret.

If, in your heart, you hold bitterness against even a single person, forgive. If there exists even one person, alive or dead, whom you have not forgiven, follow God's commandment and His will for your life: forgive. If you are embittered against yourself for some past mistake or shortcoming, forgive. Then, to the best of your abilities, forget. And move on. Bitterness and regret are not part of God's plan for your life. Forgiveness is.

Learning how to forgive and forget is one
of the secrets of a happy Christian life.

Warren Wiersbe

Forgiveness is actually the best revenge because
it not only sets us free from the person we
forgive, but it frees us to move into all
that God has in store for us.

Stormie Omartian

To hold on to hate and resentments is to throw
a monkey wrench into the machinery of life.

E. Stanley Jones

I firmly believe a great many prayers are
not answered because we are not willing
to forgive someone.

D. L. Moody

*In prayer there is a connection between what
God does and what you do. You can't get
forgiveness from God, for instance,
without also forgiving others. If you refuse
to do your part, you cut yourself off
from God's part.*

—

Matthew 6:14-15 MSG

A Prayer for Today

Lord, make me a forgiving friend.
When I am bitter, You can change my
unforgiving heart. And, when I am slow
to forgive, Your Word reminds me that
forgiveness is Your commandment.
Let me be Your obedient servant, Lord,
and let me forgive others just as
You have forgiven me.

—

Amen

CHAPTER 11

Fellowship

*How good and pleasant it is when
brothers live together in unity!*

Psalm 133:1 NIV

*F*ellowship with other believers should be an integral part of your everyday life. Your association with fellow Christians should be uplifting, enlightening, encouraging, and consistent.

Are you an active member of your own fellowship? Are you a builder of bridges inside the four walls of your church and outside it? Do you contribute to God's glory by contributing your time and your talents to a close-knit band of believers? Hopefully so.

The fellowship of believers is intended to be a powerful tool for spreading God's Good News and uplifting His children. And God intends for you to be a fully contributing member of that fellowship. *Your* intentions should be the same.

One of the ways God refills us after failure is through the blessing of Christian fellowship. Just experiencing the joy of simple activities shared with other children of God can have a healing effect on us.

Anne Graham Lotz

God shows unbridled delight when He sees people acting in ways that honor Him: when He receives worship, when He sees faith demonstrated in the most trying of circumstances, and when He sees tender love shared among His people.

Bill Hybels

And if our fellowship below in Jesus be so sweet, what greater blessings shall we know when 'round His throne we meet?

Charles Wesley

Christian brotherhood is not an ideal which we must realize; it is rather a reality created by God in Christ in which we may participate.

Dietrich Bonhoeffer

Now I plead with you, brethren, by the name of our Lord Jesus Christ, that you all speak the same thing, and that there be no divisions among you, but that you be perfectly joined together in the same mind and in the same judgment.

—

1 Corinthians 1:10 NKJV

A Prayer for Today

Lord, so much more can be accomplished when we join together to fulfill our common goals and desires. As I seek to fulfill Your will for my life, let me also join with others to accomplish Your greater good for our nation and for all humanity.

—

Amen

CHAPTER 12

The Rule That Is Golden

*So in everything, do to others what you
would have them do to you,
for this sums up the Law and the Prophets.*

Matthew 7:12 NIV

The words of Matthew 7:12 remind us that, as believers in Christ, we are commanded to treat others as we wish to be treated. This commandment is, indeed, the Golden Rule for Christians of every generation.

Kindness is a choice. Sometimes, when we feel happy or prosperous, we find it easy to be kind. Other times, when we are discouraged or tired, we can scarcely summon the energy to utter a single kind word. But, God's commandment is clear: we must observe the Golden Rule "in everything." God intends that we make the conscious choice to treat others with kindness and respect, no matter our circumstances, no matter our emotions. Kindness, therefore, is a choice that we, as Christians, must make many times each day.

When we weave the thread of kindness into the very fabric of our lives, we give a priceless gift to others, *and* we give glory to the One who gave His life for us. As believers, we must do no less.

The Golden Rule starts at home,
but it should never stop there.

Marie T. Freeman

Do all the good you can.
By all the means you can.
In all the ways you can.
In all the places you can.
At all the times you can.
To all the people you can.
As long as ever you can.

John Wesley

Love is an attribute of God.
To love others is evidence of a genuine faith.

Kay Arthur

Be so preoccupied with good will
that you haven't room for ill will.

E. Stanley Jones

And let us not be weary in well doing:
for in due season we shall reap, if we faint not.

—

Galatians 6:9 KJV

A Prayer for Today

Dear Lord, I thank You for friends and family
members who practice the Golden Rule.
Because I expect to be treated with kindness,
let me be kind. Because I wish to be loved, let
me be loving. Because I need forgiveness,
let me be merciful. In all things, Lord,
let me live by the Golden Rule, and let me
express my gratitude to those who offer
kindness and generosity to me.

—

Amen

CHAPTER 13

A Friend Is . . .

You are my friends if you do what I command.
I no longer call you servants, because a servant
does not know his master's business. Instead,
I have called you friends, for everything that
I learned from my Father I have made
known to you.

John 15:14-15 NIV

*F*riend: a one-syllable word describing "a person who is attached to another by feelings of affection or personal regard." This definition, or one very similar to it, can be found in any dictionary, but genuine friendship is much more. When we examine the deeper meaning of friendship, so many descriptors come to mind: trustworthiness, loyalty, helpfulness, kindness, understanding, forgiveness, encouragement, humor, and cheerfulness, to mention but a few.

Genuine friendship should be treasured and nurtured. As Christians, we are commanded to love one another. The familiar words of 1 Corinthians 13:2 remind us that love and charity are among God's greatest gifts: "And though I have the gift of prophecy, and understand all mysteries, and all knowledge; and though I have all faith, so that I could remove mountains, and have not charity, I am nothing" (KJV).

Today and every day, resolve to be a trustworthy, encouraging, loyal friend. And, treasure the people in your life who are loyal friends to you. Friendship is, after all, a glorious gift, praised by God. Give thanks for that gift and nurture it.

A friend is one who makes me do my best.

Oswald Chambers

Yes, the Spirit was sent to be our Counselor.
Yes, Jesus speaks to us personally.
But often he works through
another human being.

John Eldredge

Friendship is one of the sweetest joys of life.
Many might have failed beneath the bitterness
of their trial had they not found a friend.

C. H. Spurgeon

We long to find someone who has been where
we've been, who shares our fragile skies,
who sees our sunsets with
the same shades of blue.

Beth Moore

A friend loves you all the time . . .

—

Proverbs 17:17 NCV

A Prayer for Today

Lord, You seek abundance and joy for me
and for all Your children. One way that I can
share Your joy is through the gift of friendship.
Help me to be a loyal friend. Let me be ready to
listen, ready to encourage, and ready to offer
a helping hand. Keep me mindful that I am
a servant of Your Son Jesus. Let me be
a worthy servant, Lord, and a worthy friend.
And, may the love of Jesus shine through me
today and forever.

—

Amen

CHAPTER 14

Relationships That Are Built Upon Trust

*Lead a quiet and peaceable life in
all godliness and honesty.*
1 Timothy 2:2 KJV

*L*asting relationships are built upon a firm foundation of honesty and trust. Temporary relationships are built upon the shifting sands of deception and insincerity. Which foundation will you choose?

It has been said on many occasions that honesty is the best policy. But for Christians, it is far more important to note that honesty is *God's* policy. And if we are to be servants worthy of our Savior, we must be honest and forthright in all our communications with others.

Sometimes, honesty is difficult; sometimes, honesty is painful; sometimes, honesty makes us feel uncomfortable. Despite these temporary feelings of discomfort, we must make honesty the hallmark of all our relationships; otherwise, we invite needless suffering into our own lives *and* into the lives of those we love.

Sometime soon, perhaps even today, you will be tempted to bend the truth or to break it. Resist that temptation. Truth is God's way . . . and it must be your way, too.

The single most important element in any
human relationship is honesty—with oneself,
with God, and with others.

Catherine Marshall

Honesty has a beautiful and refreshing
simplicity about it. No ulterior motives.
No hidden meanings. As honesty and integrity
characterize our lives, there will be no need
to manipulate others.

Charles Swindoll

Integrity is not a given factor in everyone's life.
It is a result of self-discipline, inner trust,
and a decision to be relentlessly honest
in all situations in our lives.

John Maxwell

God doesn't expect you to be perfect,
but he does insist on complete honesty.

Rick Warren

> *Good people will be guided by honesty.*
>
> ---
>
> *Proverbs 11:3* NCV

A Prayer for Today

Lord, sometimes it's hard to tell the truth.
But even when telling the truth is difficult,
let me follow Your commandment.
Honesty isn't just *the best* policy, Lord;
it's *Your* policy, and I will obey You
by making it *my* policy, too.

—

Amen

My Thoughts & Prayers
from This Week

_____

_____

_____

_____

_____

_____

_____

_____

_____

_____

_____

_____

_____

_____

_____

_____

_____

_____

_____

_____

_____

_____

_____

My Thoughts & Prayers
for Next Week

CHAPTER 15

A Thankful Spirit

*Everything created by God is good, and nothing
is to be rejected, if it is received with gratitude;
for it is sanctified by means of the word of God
and prayer.*

1 Timothy 4:4-5 NASB

As believing Christians, we are blessed beyond measure. God sent His only Son to die for our sins. And, God has given us the priceless gifts of eternal love and eternal life. Furthermore, God has blessed us with loving family members and loyal friends.

In response to all these blessings, we are instructed to approach our Heavenly Father with reverence and thanksgiving. But sometimes, in the crush of everyday living, we simply don't stop long enough to pause and thank our Creator for the priceless gifts He has bestowed upon us.

When we slow down and express our gratitude to the One who made us, we enrich our own lives *and* the lives of those around us. Thanksgiving should become a habit, a regular part of our daily routines. God has blessed us beyond measure, and we owe Him everything, including our eternal praise.

Think of the blessings we so easily take for
granted: Life itself; preservation from danger;
every bit of health we enjoy; every hour of
liberty; the ability to see, to hear, to speak,
to think, and to imagine all this
comes from the hand of God.

Billy Graham

Nobody who gets enough food and clothing
in a world where most are hungry and
cold has any business to talk about "misery."

C. S. Lewis

It is only with gratitude that life becomes rich.

Dietrich Bonhoeffer

If you pause to think—
you'll have cause to thank!

Anonymous

As you therefore have received Christ Jesus the Lord, so walk in Him, having been firmly rooted and now being built up in Him and established in your faith, just as you were instructed, and overflowing with gratitude.

Colossians 2:6-7 NASB

A Prayer for Today

Lord, let my attitude be one of gratitude. You have given me much; when I think of Your grace and goodness, I am humbled and thankful. Today, let me express my thanksgiving, Father, not just through my words but also through my deeds . . . and may all the glory be Yours.

—

Amen

CHAPTER 16

Finding Contentment

I've learned by now to be quite content whatever my circumstances. I'm just as happy with little as with much, with much as with little. I've found the recipe for being happy whether full or hungry, hands full or hands empty.

Philippians 4:11-12 MSG

*D*o you seek happiness, abundance, and contentment? If so, here are some things you should do: Love God and His Son; depend upon God for strength; try, to the best of your abilities, to follow God's will; and strive to obey His Holy Word. When you do these things, you'll discover that happiness goes hand-in-hand with righteousness. The happiest people are not those who rebel against God; the happiest people are those who love God and obey His commandments.

What does life have in store for you and your loved ones? A world full of possibilities (of course, it's up to you to seize them), and God's promise of abundance (of course, it's up to you to accept it). So, as you embark upon the next phase of your journey, remember to celebrate the life that God has given you (and while you're at it, encourage your family and friends to do the same). Your Creator has blessed you beyond measure. Honor Him with your prayers, your words, your deeds, and your joy.

We will never be happy until we make God
the source of our fulfillment and
the answer to our longings.

Stormie Omartian

I am truly happy with Jesus Christ.
I couldn't live without Him.

Ruth Bell Graham

Joy comes not from what we have
but from what we are.

C. H. Spurgeon

Smile—it increases your face value.

Anonymous

A happy heart is like good medicine.

—

Proverbs 17:22 NCV

A Prayer for Today

Dear Lord, I am thankful for all the blessings You have given me. Let me be a happy Christian, Father, as I share Your joy with friends, with family, and with the world.

—

Amen

CHAPTER 17

Neighbors

Jesus said unto him, Thou shalt love the Lord
thy God with all thy heart, and with all thy soul,
and with all thy mind. This is the first and great
commandment. And the second is like unto it,
Thou shalt love thy neighbor as thyself.
On these two commandments hang
all the law and the prophets.

Matthew 22:37-40 KJV

*N*eighbors. We know that we are instructed to love them, and yet there's so little time . . . and we're so busy. No matter. As Christians, we are commanded by our Lord and Savior Jesus Christ to love our neighbors just as we love ourselves. We are not asked to love our neighbors, nor are we encouraged to do so. We are commanded to love them. Period.

This very day, you will encounter someone who needs a word of encouragement or a pat on the back or a helping hand or a heartfelt prayer. And, if you don't reach out to that person, who will? If you don't take the time to understand the needs of your neighbors, who will? If you don't love your brothers and sisters, who will? So, today, look for a neighbor in need . . . and then do something to help. Father's orders.

A person who really cares about his or her
neighbor, a person who genuinely loves others,
is a person who bears witness to the truth.

Anne Graham Lotz

That's a good part of the good old days—
to be genuinely interested in your neighbor,
and if you hear a distress signal,
go see about him and his problem.

Jerry Clower

Wise Christians will be generous with
their neighbors and live peaceably with them.

Warren Wiersbe

If my heart is right with God,
every human being is my neighbor.

Oswald Chambers

Therefore laying aside falsehood, speak truth,
each one of you, with his neighbor,
for we are members of one another.

—

Ephesians 4:25 NASB

A Prayer for Today

Dear Lord, the Golden Rule is a perfect
standard to use with my friends and neighbors.
Help me to treat others as I wish to be treated.
Let me be kind, fair, respectful, and generous.
In all my dealings, let me be guided by
the example of Christ so that I might glorify
Your Son through my words, my deeds,
my love for others . . . and my love for Him.

—

Amen

CHAPTER 18

Too Quick to Judge

Do not judge, and you will not be judged.
Do not condemn, and you will not be condemned.
Forgive, and you will be forgiven.

Luke 6:37 HCSB

*E*ven the most loyal Christian friends may be quick to judge and slow to forgive. We human beings, imperfect as we are, seem all too quick to judge the actions and motivations of others. The temptation to judge is both powerful and subtle, but as Christians, we are commanded to refrain from such behavior. The warning of Matthew 7:1 is clear: "Judge not, that ye be not judged." But, as fallible, imperfect human beings living in a stressful world, we are sorely tempted to do otherwise.

As Jesus came upon a young woman who had been condemned by the Pharisees, He spoke not only to the crowd that was gathered there, but also to all generations when He warned, "He that is without sin among you, let him first cast a stone at her" (John 8:7 KJV). Christ's message is clear, and it applies not only to the Pharisees of ancient times, but also to us.

We have all fallen short of God's commandments, and none of us, therefore, are qualified to "cast the first stone." Thankfully, God has forgiven us. We, too, must forgive others. When we do, we not only obey the commandment of our Creator, but we also free ourselves from the chains of bitterness and regret.

I firmly believe a great many prayers
are not answered because we are not willing
to forgive someone.

D. L. Moody

God forgets the past. Imitate him.

Max Lucado

Christians think they are prosecuting attorneys
or judges, when, in reality,
God has called all of us to be witnesses.

Warren Wiersbe

Is there somebody who's always
getting your goat?
Talk to the Shepherd.

Anonymous

Why do you look at the speck of sawdust in your brother's eye and pay no attention to the plank in your own eye? How can you say to your brother, "Let me take the speck out of your eye," when all the time there is a plank in your own eye? You hypocrite, first take the plank out of your own eye, and then you will see clearly to remove the speck from your brother's eye.

—

Matthew 7:3-5 NIV

A Prayer for Today

Lord, it's so easy to judge other people,
but it's also easy to misjudge them.
Only You can judge a human heart, Lord,
so let me love my friends and neighbors,
and let me help them,
but never let me judge them.

—

Amen

CHAPTER 19

The Heart of a Servant

Jesus sat down and called the twelve apostles
to him. He said, "Whoever wants to be the most
important must be last of all and servant of all."

Mark 9:35 NCV

We live in a world that glorifies power, prestige, fame, and money. But the words of Jesus teach us that the most esteemed men and women in this world are not the self-congratulatory leaders of society but are instead the humblest of servants.

Today, you may feel the temptation to build yourself up in the eyes of your friends and neighbors. Resist that temptation. Instead, serve your neighbors quietly and without fanfare. Find a need and fill it . . . humbly. Lend a helping hand . . . anonymously. Share a word of kindness . . . with quiet sincerity. As you go about your daily activities, remember that the Savior of all humanity made Himself a servant, and we, as His followers, must do no less.

I have discovered that when I please Christ,
I end up inadvertently serving others
far more effectively.

Beth Moore

There are times when we are called to love,
expecting nothing in return. There are times
when we are called to give money to people
who will never say thanks, to forgive those who
won't forgive us, to come early and stay late
when no one else notices.

Max Lucado

If the attitude of servanthood is learned,
by attending to God as Lord.
Then, serving others will develop
as a very natural way of life.

Eugene Peterson

I can usually sense that a leading is from the
Holy Spirit when it calls me to humble myself,
serve somebody, encourage somebody or give
something away. Very rarely will the evil one
lead us to do those kinds of things.

Bill Hybels

*But he who is greatest among you
shall be your servant.*

—

Matthew 23:11 NKJV

A Prayer for Today

Dear Lord, give me a servant's heart.
When Jesus humbled Himself and
became a servant, He also became
an example for His followers.
Make me a faithful steward of my gifts,
and let me share with those in need.

—

Amen

CHAPTER 20

Pleasing God First

Do you think I am trying to make people accept me?
No, God is the One I am trying to please.
Am I trying to please people? If I still wanted to
please people, I would not be a servant of Christ.

Galatians 1:10 NCV

*I*f you're like most people, you're anxious to please your friends . . . but you shouldn't be *too* anxious to please them. Instead, you should always seek to please God first.

Obedience to God is determined, not by words, but by deeds. Talking about righteousness is easy; living righteously and responsibly is far more difficult, especially in today's temptation-filled world.

When Jesus was tempted by Satan, the Master's response was unambiguous. Jesus chose to worship the Lord and serve Him only. We, as followers of Christ, must follow in His footsteps. When we place God in a position of secondary importance, we do ourselves great harm. But, when we imitate Jesus and place the Lord in His rightful place—at the center of our lives—then we claim spiritual treasures that will endure forever.

Whom will you try to please today: God or man? Your primary obligation is not to please imperfect men and women. Your obligation is to strive diligently to meet the expectations of an all-knowing and perfect God. Trust Him always. Love Him always. Praise Him always. And seek to please Him. Always.

Fashion is an enduring testimony to the fact
that we live quite consciously
before the eyes of others.

John Eldredge

When we are set free from the bondage of
pleasing others, when we are free from currying
others' favor and others' approval—then no one
will be able to make us miserable or dissatisfied.
And then, if we know we have pleased God,
contentment will be our consolation.

Kay Arthur

It is comfortable to know that we are
responsible to God and not to man.
It is a small matter to be judged
of man's judgement.

Lottie Moon

Those who follow the crowd usually
get lost in it.

Rick Warren

> *Do not be fooled:*
> *"Bad friends will ruin good habits."*
>
> —
>
> 1 Corinthians 15:33 NCV

A Prayer for Today

Dear Lord, today I will worry less about pleasing
other people and more about pleasing You.
I will honor You with my thoughts, my actions,
and my prayers. And I will worship You, Father,
with thanksgiving in my heart,
this day and forever.

—

Amen

CHAPTER 21

A God of Infinite Possibilities

*No eye has seen, no ear has heard,
no mind has conceived what God has prepared
for those who love him.*

1 Corinthians 2:9 NIV

ometimes, because we are imperfect human beings with limited understanding and limited faith, we place limitations on God. But, God's power has no such limitations. God is perfectly willing and perfectly able to work miracles in our own lives *and* in the lives of our family members and friends. In fact, miracles, both great and small, are an integral part of everyday life, but usually, we are too busy or too cynical to notice God's handiwork. We don't expect to see miracles, so we simply overlook them.

Do you lack the faith that God can do miraculous things for you and your loved ones? If so, it's time to reconsider. If you have allowed yourself to become a "doubting Thomas," you are attempting to place limitations on a God who has none. Instead of doubting your Heavenly Father, you must trust Him. Then, you must wait and watch . . . because something miraculous is going to happen, and it might just happen today.

There is Someone who makes possible
what seems completely impossible.

Catherine Marshall

If all things are possible with God,
then all things are possible to him
who believes in him.

Corrie ten Boom

When you believe that nothing significant
can happen through you, you have said
more about your belief in God
than you have said about yourself.

Henry Blackaby

When we face an impossible situation,
all self-reliance and self-confidence must
melt away; we must be totally dependent
on Him for the resources.

Anne Graham Lotz

For with God nothing will be impossible.

—

Luke 1:37 NKJV

A Prayer for Today

Dear God, nothing is impossible for You.
Your infinite power is beyond human
understanding—keep me always mindful of
Your strength. When I lose hope, give me faith;
when others lose hope, let me tell them of
Your glory and Your works. Today, Lord,
let me expect the miraculous,
and let me trust in You.

—

Amen

My Thoughts & Prayers
from This Week

_____

_____

_____

_____

_____

_____

_____

_____

_____

_____

_____

_____

_____

_____

_____

_____

_____

_____

_____

_____

_____

My Thoughts & Prayers
for Next Week

CHAPTER 22

Healthy Relationships

He who walks with the wise grows wise . . . .
Proverbs 13:20 NIV

*E*motional health is contagious, and so is emotional distress. If you're fortunate enough to be surrounded by family members and friends who celebrate life and praise God, consider yourself profoundly blessed. But, if you find yourself caught in an unhealthy relationship, it's time to look realistically at your situation and begin making changes.

Don't worry about changing other people: you can't do it. What you *can* do is to conduct yourself in a responsible fashion and insist that other people treat you with the dignity and consideration that you deserve.

In a perfect world filled with perfect people, our relationships, too, would be perfect. But none of us are perfect, and neither are our relationships . . . and that's okay. As we work to make our imperfect relationships a little happier and healthier, we grow as individuals and as families. But, if we find ourselves in relationships that are debilitating or dangerous, then changes must be made, and soon.

God has grand plans for your life; He has promised you the joy and abundance that can be yours through Him. But to fully experience

God's gifts, you need happy, emotionally healthy people to share them with. It's up to you to make sure that you do *your* part to build the kinds of relationships that will bring abundance to you, to your family, and to God's world.

It is possible to be close to people physically and miles away from them spiritually.

Warren Wiersbe

I don't buy the cliché that quality time is the most important thing. If you don't have enough quantity, you won't get quality.

Leighton Ford

Line by line, moment by moment, special times are etched into our memories in the permanent ink of everlasting love in our relationships.

Gloria Gaither

*Do not be unequally yoked together with
unbelievers. For what fellowship has
righteousness with lawlessness?
And what communion has light with darkness?*

—

2 Corinthians 6:14 NKJV

A Prayer for Today

Dear Lord, You have brought family members
and friends into my life. Let me love them,
let me help them, let me treasure them,
and let me lead them to You.

—

Amen

CHAPTER 23

The Ultimate Friend

Greater love has no one than this,
that he lay down his life for his friends.

John 15:13 NIV

*J*esus loved you so much that He endured unspeakable humiliation and suffering for you. How will you respond to Christ's sacrifice? Will you take up His cross and follow Him (Luke 9:23), or will you choose another path? When you place your hopes squarely at the foot of the cross, when you place Jesus squarely at the center of your life, you will be blessed.

Nineteenth-century writer Hannah Whitall Smith observed, "The crucial question for each of us is this: What do you think of Jesus, and do you yet have a personal acquaintance with Him?" Indeed, the answer to that question determines the quality, the course, and the direction of our lives today and for all eternity.

The old familiar hymn begins, "What a friend we have in Jesus . . . ." No truer words were ever penned. Jesus is the ultimate friend and savior of mankind. Christ showed enduring love for His believers by willingly sacrificing His own life so that we might have eternal life. Now, it is our turn to become His friend.

Let us love our Savior, praise Him, and share His message of salvation with our neighbors and with the world. When we do, we demonstrate that our acquaintance with the Master is not a passing fancy; it is, instead, the cornerstone and the touchstone of our lives.

As we make an offering of our work,
we find the truth of a principle Jesus taught:
Fulfillment is not a goal to achieve,
but always the by-product of a sacrifice.

Elisabeth Elliot

The secret of the Christian is that he knows the absolute deity of the Lord Jesus Christ.

Oswald Chambers

This is love: not that we loved God,
but that he loved us and sent his Son
as an atoning sacrifice for our sins.

—

1 John 4:10 NIV

A Prayer for Today

Thank You, Lord, for Your Son Jesus,
the Savior of my life. You loved this world
so dearly, Father, that You sent Your Son to
die so that we, Your children, might have life
eternal. Let me be ever grateful for that priceless
gift, and let the love of Jesus be reflected
in my words, my thoughts, and my deeds.
Let me always count Jesus as my dearest friend,
and let me share His transforming message
with a world in desperate need of His peace.

—

Amen

CHAPTER 24

Being Patient With Others . . . Being Patient With Ourselves

. . . He [God] who began a good work in you will carry it on to completion . . . .

Philippians 1:6 NIV

*B*eing patient with other people can be difficult. But sometimes, we find it even more difficult to be patient with ourselves. We have high expectations and lofty goals. We want to accomplish things now, not later. And, of course, we want our lives to unfold according to our own timetables, not God's.

Throughout the Bible, we are instructed that patience is the companion of wisdom. Proverbs 16:32 teaches us that "Patience is better than strength" (NCV). And, in 1 Peter 5:6, we are told to "humble yourselves under the mighty hand of God, that He may exalt you in due time" (NKJV).

God's message, then, is clear: we must be patient with *all* people, beginning with that particular person who stares back at us each time we gaze into the mirror.

We must learn to wait.
There is grace supplied to the one who waits.

Mrs. Charles E. Cowman

Being loved by Him whose opinion matters
most gives us the security to risk loving, too—
even loving ourselves.

Gloria Gaither

The next time you're disappointed,
don't panic and don't give up. Just be patient
and let God remind you he's still in control.

Max Lucado

The times we find ourselves having to wait on
others may be the perfect opportunities
to train ourselves to wait on the Lord.

Joni Eareckson Tada

A patient heart is better than a tranquilizer.

Marie T. Freeman

We urge you, brethren, admonish the unruly,
encourage the fainthearted, help the weak,
be patient with everyone.

—

1 Thessalonians 5:14 NASB

A Prayer for Today

Heavenly Father, give me patience. Let me live according to Your plan and according to Your timetable. When I am hurried, slow me down. When I become impatient with others, give me empathy. When I am frustrated by the demands of the day, give me peace. Today, let me be a patient Christian, Dear Lord, as I trust in You and in Your master plan for my life.

—

Amen

CHAPTER 25

Sharing

*If you have two coats, give one to the poor.
If you have food,
share it with those who are hungry.*

Luke 3:11 NLT

We live in a fast-paced, competitive world where it is easy to say, "Me first." But, God instructs us to do otherwise. In God's kingdom, those who proclaim, "Me first," are last. God loves a cheerful, selfless giver.

Sometimes, amid the distractions and busyness of everyday living, we may fail to share our possessions, our talents, or our time. Yet, God commands that we treat others as we wish to be treated. God's Word makes it clear: we must be generous with others just as we seek generosity for ourselves.

As believers in Christ, we are blessed here on earth, and we are blessed eternally through God's grace. We can never fully repay God for His gifts, but we can share them with others. When we give sacrificially, our blessings are multiplied . . . and so is our joy.

Nothing is really ours until we share it.

C. S. Lewis

God shows unbridled delight when He sees people acting in ways that honor Him: when He receives worship, when He sees faith demonstrated in the most trying of circumstances, and when He sees tender love shared among His people.

Bill Hybels

Our faith grows by expression.
If we want to keep our faith, we must share it.
We must act.

Billy Graham

The best times in life are made a thousand times better when shared with a dear friend.

Luci Swindoll

The righteous give without sparing.

—

Proverbs 21:26 NIV

A Prayer for Today

Lord, I know there is no happiness in keeping Your blessings for myself. True joy is found in sharing what I have with others. Make me a generous, loving, humble servant, Dear Lord, as I follow the example of Your Son Jesus.

—

Amen

CHAPTER 26

The Words That We Speak

When you talk, do not say harmful things, but say what people need—words that will help others become stronger. Then what you say will do good to those who listen to you.

Ephesians 4:29 NCV

In the Book of Proverbs, we read that, "A word aptly spoken is like apples of gold in settings of silver" (25:11 NIV). This verse reminds us that the words we speak can and should be beautiful offerings to those who hear them.

All of us have the power to enrich the lives of others. Sometimes, when we feel uplifted and secure, it is easy to speak words of encouragement and hope. Other times, when we are discouraged or tired, we can scarcely summon the energy to pick *ourselves* up, much less anyone else. But, as loving Christians, our obligation is clear: we must always measure our words carefully as we use them to benefit others.

God intends that we speak words of kindness, wisdom, and truth, no matter our circumstances, no matter our emotions. When we do, we share a priceless gift with the world, and we honor the One who gave His life for us.

Fill the heart with the love of Christ
so that only truth and purity can come
out of the mouth.

Warren Wiersbe

I still believe we ought to talk about Jesus.
The old country doctor of my boyhood days
always began his examination by saying,
"Let me see your tongue." That's a good way
to check a Christian: the tongue test.
Let's hear what he is talking about.

Vance Havner

When you talk, choose the very same words
that you would use if Jesus were
looking over your shoulder. Because He is.

Marie T. Freeman

The things that we feel most deeply we ought to
learn to be silent about, at least until we have
talked them over thoroughly with God.

Elisabeth Elliot

*For out of the overflow of the heart
the mouth speaks.*

—

Matthew 12:34 NIV

A Prayer for Today

Lord, You have warned me that I will be
judged by the words I speak. And, You have
commanded me to choose my words carefully
so that I might be a source of encouragement
and hope to others. Keep me mindful, Lord,
that I have influence on many people . . .
make me an influence for good. And may
the words that I speak today be worthy of
the One who has saved me forever.

—

Amen

CHAPTER 27

Beyond Perfectionism

Those who wait for perfect weather will never plant seeds; those who look at every cloud will never harvest crops. Plant early in the morning, and work until evening, because you don't know if this or that will succeed. They might both do well.

Ecclesiastes 11:4, 6 NCV

*E*xpectations, expectations, expectations! The media delivers an endless stream of messages that tell you and your friends how to look, how to behave, and how to dress. The media's expectations are impossible to meet—God's are not. God doesn't expect perfection . . . and neither should you.

If you find yourself bound up by the chains of perfectionism, it's time to ask yourself whom you're trying to impress, and why. If you're trying to impress other people, it's time to reconsider your priorities. Your first responsibility is to the Heavenly Father who created you and to His Son who saved you. Then, you bear a powerful responsibility to your family. But, when it comes to meeting society's unrealistic expectations, forget it!

Remember that when you accepted Christ as your Savior, God accepted you for all eternity. Now, it's your turn to accept yourself *and* your loved ones. When you do, you'll feel a tremendous weight being lifted from your shoulders. After all, pleasing God is simply a matter of obeying His commandments and accepting His Son. But as for pleasing everybody else? That's impossible!

We shall never come to the perfect man
til we come to the perfect world.

Matthew Henry

What makes a Christian a Christian is not
perfection but forgiveness.

Max Lucado

The happiest people in the world are not those
who have no problems, but the people who
have learned to live with those things
that are less than perfect.

James Dobson

God is so inconceivably good.
He's not looking for perfection.
He already saw it in Christ.
He's looking for affection.

Beth Moore

*People are happy if they can do
what they think is right without feeling guilty.*

—

Romans 14:22 NCV

A Prayer for Today

Dear Lord, You have taught us that love covers
a multitude of shortcomings. Keep us mindful
that perfection will be ours in the next world,
not in this one. Help us to be accepting of our
own imperfections, and give us the wisdom
to accept—and even to cherish—
the imperfections of those we love.

—

Amen

CHAPTER 28

Encouraging Words for Difficult Days

*A wise man will hear and increase in learning, and
a man of understanding will acquire wise counsel.*

Proverbs 1:5 NASB

We live in a world that is, on occasion, a frightening place. Sometimes, we sustain life-changing losses that are so profound and so tragic that it seems we could never recover. But, with God's help and with the help of encouraging family members and friends, we can recover.

In times of need, friends comfort friends. Our task, as Christians, is to comfort our families and friends by sharing not only our own courage but also the peace and assurance of our Lord and Savior, Christ Jesus.

In times of adversity, we are wise to remember the words of Jesus who, when He walked on the waters, reassured His disciples, saying, "Take courage! It is I. Don't be afraid" (Matthew 14:27 NIV). Then, with Christ on His throne and trusted friends at our side, we can face our fears with courage and faith.

God guides through the counsel of good people.

E. Stanley Jones

The true secret of giving advice is,
after you've given it, to be perfectly indifferent
as to whether it is taken or not.

Hannah Whitall Smith

Make it a rule, and pray to God to help you to
keep it, never, if possible, to lie down at night
without being able to say: "I have made
one human being at least a little wiser, or a little
happier, or at least a little better this day."

Charles Kingsley

It takes a wise person to give good advice,
but an even wiser person to take it.

Marie T. Freeman

> *Timely advice is as lovely as golden apples in a silver basket.*
>
> —
>
> *Proverbs 25:11* NLT

A Prayer for Today

Lord, make me a wise counselor to those whom I teach. Make me a worthy mentor and a godly example to my friends. Let me lead them in the ways of wisdom, discipline, and righteousness by the words that I speak and the way that I live my life.

—

Amen

My Thoughts & Prayers
from This Week

My Thoughts & Prayers
for Next Week

_____

_____

_____

_____

_____

_____

_____

_____

_____

_____

_____

_____

_____

_____

_____

_____

_____

_____

_____

_____

_____

_____

CHAPTER 29

His Peace

Peace I leave with you, My peace I give to you;
not as the world gives do I give to you.
Let not your heart be troubled,
neither let it be afraid.

John 14:27 NKJV

The beautiful words of John 14:27 give us hope: "Peace I leave with you, my peace I give unto you . . . ." Jesus offers us peace, not as the world gives, but as He alone gives. We, as believers, can accept His peace or ignore it.

When we accept the peace of Jesus Christ into our hearts, our lives are transformed. And then, because we possess the gift of peace, we can share that gift with fellow Christians, family members, friends, and associates. If, on the other hand, we choose to ignore the gift of peace—for whatever reason—we simply cannot share what we do not possess.

Today, as a gift to yourself, to your family, and to your friends, claim the inner peace that is your spiritual birthright: the peace of Jesus Christ. It is offered freely; it has been paid for in full; it is yours for the asking. So ask. And then share.

"My peace I give unto you"; it is a peace all over
from the crown of the head to the sole of
the feet, an irrepressible confidence.

Oswald Chambers

The things we think are the things that feed
our souls. If we think on pure and lovely things,
we shall grow pure and lovely like them;
and the converse is equally true.

Hannah Whitall Smith

Peace does not mean to be in a place where
there is no noise, trouble, or hard work.
Peace means to be in the midst of all those
things and still be calm in your heart.

Catherine Marshall

Peace with God is where all peace begins.

Jim Gallery

And the peace of God, which surpasses every thought, will guard your hearts and your minds in Christ Jesus. Finally brothers, whatever is true, whatever is honorable, whatever is just, whatever is pure, whatever is lovely, whatever is commendable—if there is any moral excellence and if there is any praise—dwell on these things.

—

Philippians 4:7-8 HCSB

A Prayer for Today

Dear Lord, the peace that the world offers is fleeting, but You offer a peace that is perfect and eternal. Let me take my concerns and burdens to You, Father, and let me feel the spiritual abundance that You offer through the person of Your Son, the Prince of Peace.

—

Amen

CHAPTER 30

Walking
in Truth

*I have no greater joy than this,
to hear of my children walking in the truth.*

3 John 1:4 NASB

*G*od's Holy Word instructs us that Jesus said, "I am the way, the truth, and the life. No one comes to the Father except through Me. If you had known Me, you would have known My Father also; and from now on you know Him and have seen Him" (John 14: 6-7 NKJV).

Without Christ, we can never know the ultimate truth: *God's* truth.

Truth is God's way: He commands His believers to live in truth, and He rewards those who do so. Jesus is the personification of God's liberating truth, a truth that offers salvation to mankind.

Do you seek to walk with God? Do you seek to feel His presence and His peace? Then you must walk in truth, and you must walk with the Savior. There is simply no other way.

For Christians, God himself is the only absolute;
truth and ethics are rooted in his character.

Chuck Colson

Peace, if possible, but truth at any rate.

Martin Luther

Truth will triumph.
The Father of truth will win,
and the followers of truth will be saved.

Max Lucado

The temple of truth has never suffered
so much from the wood peckers on
the outside as from termites within.

Vance Havner

> *And you shall know the truth,*
> *and the truth shall make you free.*
>
> —
>
> *John 8:32 NKJV*

A Prayer for Today

Dear Lord, Jesus said He is the truth,
and I believe Him. Father, may Jesus always
be the standard for truth in my life so that
I might be a worthy example to others
and a worthy servant to You.

—

Amen

CHAPTER 31

Loving God . . . With All Your Heart

I love you, O LORD, my strength.
Psalm 18:1 NIV

*C*hrist's words left no room for interpretation: "'Love the Lord your God with all your heart and with all your soul and with all your mind.' This is the first and greatest commandment. And the second is like it: 'Love your neighbor as yourself.' All the Law and the Prophets hang on these two commandments" (Matthew 22:37-40 NIV). But sometimes, despite our best intentions, we fall short. When we become embittered with ourselves, with our neighbors, or most especially with God, we disobey the One who gave His life for us.

If we are to please God, we must cleanse ourselves of the negative feelings that separate us from others and from Him. In 1 Corinthians 13, we are told that love is the foundation upon which all our relationships are to be built: our relationships with others and our relationship with our Maker. May we fill our hearts with love; may we never yield to bitterness. And may we praise the Son of God who, in His infinite wisdom, made love His greatest commandment.

If you want to know the will and voice of God,
you must give the time and effort to cultivate
a love relationship with Him.
That is what He wants!

Henry Blackaby

In the long run there will be but two kinds
of men: those who love God
and those who love something else.

St. Augustine

If you love God enough to ask Him what
you can do for *Him*, then your relationship is
growing deep.

Stormie Omartian

What is Christian perfection?
Loving God with all our heart, mind, soul,
and strength.

John Wesley

We love Him because He first loved us.

—

1 John 4:19 NKJV

A Prayer for Today

Dear Heavenly Father, You have blessed me
with a love that is infinite and eternal.
Let me love You, Lord, more and more each day.
Make me a loving servant, Father, today and
throughout eternity. And, let me show my love
for You by sharing Your message
and Your love with others.

—

Amen

My Thoughts & Prayers
for the Month

_____

_____

_____

_____

_____

_____

_____

_____

_____

_____

_____

_____

_____

_____

_____

_____

_____

_____

_____

_____

_____

_____

My Thoughts & Prayers
for the Month

Bible Verses to Consider

Kindness

Be kindly affectionate to one another with brotherly love, in honor giving preference to one another; not lagging in diligence, fervent in spirit, serving the Lord; rejoicing in hope, patient in tribulation, continuing steadfastly in prayer.

Romans 12:10-12 NKJV

Here is a simple, rule-of-thumb for behavior: Ask yourself what you want people to do for you, then grab the initiative and do it for them. Add up God's Law and Prophets and this is what you get.

Matthew 7:12 MSG

Assuredly, I say to you, inasmuch as you did it to one of the least of these My brethren, you did it to Me.

Matthew 25:40 NKJV

Be kind to one another, tender-hearted, forgiving each other, just as God in Christ also has forgiven you.

Ephesians 4:32 NASB

Carry each other's burdens,
and in this way you will fulfill
the law of Christ.

—

Galatians 6:2 NIV

Honesty

The LORD detests lying lips,
but he delights in men who are truthful.

Proverbs 12:22 NIV

So put away all falsehood and
"tell your neighbor the truth"
because we belong to each other.

Ephesians 4:25 NLT

Lead a quiet and peaceable life
in all godliness and honesty.

1 Timothy 2:2 KJV

And you shall know the truth,
and the truth shall make you free.

John 8:32 NKJV

The godly are directed
by their honesty.

—

Proverbs 11:5 NLT

God's Love

And we have known and believed the love
that God has for us. God is love, and he who abides
in love abides in God, and God in him.

1 John 4:16 NKJV

The Lord is full of compassion and mercy.

James 5:11 NIV

Praise him, all you people of the earth,
for he loves us with unfailing love; the faithfulness
of the LORD endures forever. Praise the LORD!

Psalm 117 NLT

For God so loved the world, that he gave his only
begotten Son, that whosoever believeth in him
should not perish, but have everlasting life.

John 3:16 KJV

*The unfailing love
of the Lord never ends!*

—

Lamentations 3:22 NLT

Service

*Sitting down, He called the Twelve and
said to them, "If anyone wants to be first,
he must be last of all and servant of all."*

Mark 9:35 HCSB

*But whoever desires to become great among you,
let him be your servant. And whoever desires to be
first among you, let him be your slave—just as the
Son of Man did not come to be served, but to serve,
and to give His life a ransom for many."*

Matthew 20:26-28 NKJV

*Then the righteous will answer Him, saying,
"Lord, when did we see You hungry and feed You,
or thirsty and give You drink? When did we see You
a stranger and take You in, or naked and clothe
You? Or when did we see You sick, or in prison,
and come to You?" And the King will answer and
say to them, "Assuredly, I say to you, inasmuch as
you did it to one of the least of these My brethren,
you did it to Me."*

Matthew 25:37-40 NKJV

Whatever you do, work at it with
all your heart, as working for the Lord,
not for men, since you know that
you will receive an inheritance
from the Lord as a reward.
It is the Lord Christ you are serving.

—

Colossians 3:23-24 NIV

Encouragement

Feed the flock of God which is among you . . . .

1 Peter 5:2 KJV

Finally, all of you be of one mind, having compassion for one another; love as brothers, be tenderhearted, be courteous.

1 Peter 3:8 NKJV

*Watch the way you talk.
Let nothing foul or dirty come out of your mouth.
Say only what helps, each word a gift.*

Ephesians 4:29 MSG

So encourage each other and give each other strength, just as you are doing now.

1 Thessalonians 5:11 NCV

Good people's words

will help many others.

—

Proverbs 10:21 NCV